bakkhai

bakkhai

euripides

a new version by
anne carson

a new directions book

Cover art: Ragnar Kjartansson, *The End*, 2009. Collection of Fondazione Sandretto Re Rebaudengo. Courtesy of the artist; Luhring Augustine, New York; and i8 Gallery, Reykjavik. Commissioned for the Icelandic Pavilion at the 53rd Venice Biennale: six-month performance during which 144 paintings were made.

Manufactured in the United States of America
First published clothbound by New Directions in 2017

Library of Congress Cataloging-in-Publication
Names: Euripides, author. | Carson, Anne, 1950– translator.
Title: Bakkhai / a new translation by Anne Carson.
Other titles: Bacchae. English (Carson) | Bakkhai
Description: New York : New Directions, 2017.
Identifiers: LCCN 2017018494 | ISBN 9780811227100 (alk. paper)
Subjects: LCSH: Dionysus (Greek deity)—Drama. | Pentheus, King of Thebes (Mythological character)—Drama. | Bacchantes—Drama. | GSAFD: Tragedies.
Classification: LCC PA3975.B2 C37 2017 | DDC 882/.01—dc23
LC record available at https://lccn.loc.gov/2017018494882'.01—dc2

10 9 8 7 6 5 4 3

New Directions Books are published for James Laughlin
by New Directions Publishing Corporation
80 Eighth Avenue, New York 10011

bakkhai

i wish i were two dogs then i could play with me
(translator's note on euripides' *bakkhai*)

Dionysos is god
of the beginning
before the beginning.

What makes
beginnings special?
Think of

your first sip of wine
from a really good bottle.
Opening page

of a crime novel.
Start
of an idea.

Tingle of falling in love.
Beginnings have their own
energy,

ethics,
tonality,
colour.

Greenish-bluish-purple
dewy and cool
almost transparent,

as a ripe grape.
Tone of alterity,
things just about to change,

already looking different.
Energy headlong
and heedless

and shot
like a beam. Ethics
fantastically selfish.

He is a young god.
Mythologically obscure,
always just arriving

at some new place
to disrupt the status quo,
wearing the start of a smile.

The Greeks called him "foreign"
and staged his incursion
into polis after polis

in stories like the one
in Euripides' Bakkhai.
A shocking play.

Lecturing in Japan
Stephen Hawking was asked
not to mention that the universe

had a beginning
(and so likely an end)
because it would affect

the stockmarket.
Speculation aside,
we all need a prehistory.

According to Freud,
we do nothing but repeat it.
Beginnings are special

because most of them are fake.
The new person you become
with that first sip of wine

was already there.
Look at Pentheus
twirling around in a dress,

so pleased with his girl-guise
he's almost in tears.
Are we to believe

this desire is new?
Why was he keeping
that dress in the back

of his closet anyhow?
Costume is flesh.
Look at Dionysos,

plucked prematurely
from his doomed mother's womb
and sewn up

in the thigh of Zeus
to be born again later.
Life is a rehearsal

for life.
Here's a well-known secret
about Dionysos:

despite all those legends
of him as "new god"
imported to Greece from the east,

his name is already
on Linear B tablets
that date to 12th-century BC.

Previousness
is something a god can manage
fairly well ("time"

a fiction for him)
but mortals
less so.

Look at those poor passionate women
who worship this god,
the Bakkhai,

destroyers of livestock
and local people
and Pentheus the king.

They had a prior existence once.
The herdsman describes them
lying at peace in the mountains

"calm as buttons on a shirt."
This is the world before men.
Then the posse arrives

and violence begins.
What does this tell us?
The shock of the new

will prepare its own unveiling
in old and brutal ways.
Dionysos does not

explain or regret
anything. He is
pleased

if he can cause you to perform,
despite your plan,
despite your politics,

despite your neuroses,
despite even your Dionysian theories of self,
something quite previous,

the desire
before the desire,
the lick of beginning to know you don't know.

If life is a stage,
that is the show.
Exit Dionysos.

cast

Dionysos
Teiresias
Kadmos
Pentheus
Guard
Herdsman
Servant
Agave
and
Bakkhai

PROLOGUE

[enter Dionysos]

Dionysos: Here I am.
Dionysos.
I am
son of Zeus, born by a lightning bolt out of Semele
– you know this story—
the night Zeus split her open with fire.
In order to come here I changed my form,
put on this suit of human presence.
I want to visit the springs of Dirke,
the river Ismenos.
Look there—I see
the tomb of my mother,
thunderstruck Semele,
and her ruined house still smoking
with the live flame of Zeus.
I'm glad
my grandfather Kadmos named this place sacred,
I'm glad
he keeps it clean.
I myself
planted it all round with vines
in the clear key of green.
The story so far:

I crossed Lydia, Phrygia, Baktria, Media, Arabia and
        the whole coastland of Asia
to come here
to this Greek city
to make myself known:
my rituals, my dances, my religion, my livewire self!
I am something supernatural—
not exactly god, ghost, spirit, angel, principle or
        element—
There is no term for it in English.
In Greek they say *daimon*—
can we just use that?
So,
I set all Asia dancing
and then I came here
first
of all the cities of Greece:
I came to thrill you, Thebes.
Don't doubt I will.
Here's what you'll need:
fawnskin,
thyrsos,
absolute submission.
My mother's sisters failed to understand
        this—they've
been going around saying
Dionysos wasn't born of Zeus,
Kadmos just made that up
after Semele slept with a perfectly ordinary person.
It was wrong of them to say such things.
I have stung them from their homes,
they are gone mad upon the mountains.

The whole bursting female seed-pod of Thebes is
        gone mad.
I've put them in Dionysian uniform
and they sit beneath pine trees
staring at their own green hands.
So they will learn,
so Thebes must learn,
to call me son of Zeus
and call me
daimon.

Now Thebes has a new leader.
Kadmos appointed him.
He's Kadmos' grandson. Name is Pentheus.
This man is against me.
He does not acknowledge me in libation or prayer.
But I *am* a god. I'll show him. Him and all his Thebans.
Then I'll be on my way to another land in visible
        triumph.
But if Thebes comes forth in anger
to drive my Bakkhic women from the mountains
I shall lead them as an army into battle.
That's why I've changed to mortal form—
how do I look?
Convincingly human?

O dear women! My cadre, my sisterhood, my fellow
        travellers—
you who left your distant lives
to wander all the way from Lydia with me—
lift up your tambourines!
bang loud your drums!

Surround Pentheus' house with noise and let the city
see you!
I'll go to Mt Kithairon
and get them dancing there.

[enter Bakkhai]

ENTRANCE SONG OF THE BAKKHAI

From Asia I come,

> from Tmolos I hasten,
> to this work that I love,
> to this love that I live
>> calling out
>> *Bakkhos*!
> Who is in the road?
> Who is in the way?
Stay back,
stand quiet.
I shall sing Dionysos—
> I shall make the simplest sentence explode with his name!

O
blessed is he who,
> blessedly happy is he who
>> knows the holy protocols, who
>>> makes his life pure, who
>>> joins his soul in congregation
>> on the mountains of Bakkhos!
> Honouring the Mother
and the mysteries
>>> with his thyrsos,
>>> his ivy,
>>> his submission to the god.
>> Come, Bakkhai!
>> Come Bakkhai,
>> bring your god home!
>> Bring Bromios down from the mountains of
>>>> Phrygia
into the wide dancing streets of Greece!

Bromios,
the one whose
mother shimmered into fire
at the moment of his birth
when Zeus' lightning bolt blew her apart
and Zeus sewed the infant into his own thigh
with golden stitches,
secret and safe
until the appointed time.
Then he was born
a god
with horns on his head
and snakes in his hair—
that's why
the Bakkhai
like to play with wild things even now.

O Thebes! garland yourself
in all the green there is—
ivy green,
olive green,
fennel green,
growing green,
yearning green,
wet sap green,
new grape green,
green of youth and green of branches,
green of mint and green of marsh grass,
green of tea leaves, oak and pine,
green of washed needles and early rain,
green of weeds and green of oceans,
green of bottles, ferns and apples,
green of dawn-soaked dew and slender green of roots,

green fresh out of pools,
green slipped under fools,
green of the green fuse,
green of the honeyed muse,
green of the rough caress of ritual,
green undaunted by reason or delirium,
green of jealous joy,
green of the secret holy violence of the thyrsos,
green of the sacred iridescence of the dance—
and let all the land of Thebes dance!
with Dionysos leading,
to the mountains!
to the mountains!
where the mob of women waits!
They've forsaken their shuttles,
they've left their looms,
they've dropped their aprons
and taken up their stations
on Dionysos' mountain!
He has stung them out of their minds.

Do you hear that pounding?
Do you hear the kettledrum?
The Korybants invented it
to mingle with the sweet shrill voice of the flute
and they gave it to the Mother,
who gave it to the Satyrs,
who gave it to us.
We dance to a drumbeat adoring our god.
He loves the drum!

                    He is sweet upon the mountains
                        when he runs from the pack,

when he drops to the ground,
hunting goatkill blood
and rawflesh pleasure,
longing for the mountains of home!
Bromios, leader of the dance!
EUOI!
His ground flows with milk,
flows with wine,
flows with nectar of bees.
Like smoke of incense streaming aloft
his pinetorch blazes.
He darts.
He runs.
He dances.
He touches them to fire if they lag
and rouses them with shouts if they wander,
and all the while his long hair streaming on the wind
and all the while his low voice pulsing into them,
Run, Bakkhai!
Run, Bakkhai!
You amazing golden creatures!
Sing Dionysos!
Sing glorying your god
in the thunder of drums!
To the mountains! To the mountains!
EUOI!
EUOI!
Look,
there she goes,
lost in joy,
like a colt from its mother frisking free,
the creature
of Bakkhos!

22

[enter Teiresias]

Teiresias: You at the gates!
               Call Kadmos out—go on, tell him Teiresias is here,
               he'll know why.
               We have an agreement, one old man with another,
               to try out this Dionysian business together—
               fawnskin, thyrsos, garlands in the hair—the complete
                    regalia.

[enter Kadmos from palace]

Kadmos: I knew it was you, my old wise friend,
               I heard your voice.
               Look, I've got my gear on too—the costume of the god!
               Now the important thing is
               to promote Dionysos
               every way we can,
               he's my daughter's son after all.
               So where are we headed?
               I'm ready to dance or trance or toss our white heads
               or whatever comes next.
               You lead the way, Teiresias, you're the wise one.
               I'm merely enthusiastic!
               Isn't it fun to forget our old age?

Teiresias: Yes well, what is it they say,
               you're as young as you feel?

Kadmos: We must get to the mountain.
               Should we call a cab?

Teiresias: That doesn't sound very Dionysian.

Kadmos: Good point. Let's walk. We can lean on each other.

Teiresias: The god will guide us, it won't be hard.

Kadmos: We're the only ones in the city going?

Teiresias: The only ones who have any sense.

Kadmos: No more delay then, take my hand.

Teiresias: Here we go, arm in arm.

Kadmos: I don't believe in despising the gods,
a mere human myself.

Teiresias: And I don't believe in philosophizing about it.
We know he's a *daimon*,
we know there are certain traditions pertaining to
that,
traditions as old as time,
why analyze further?
What wisdom is in it?
Will they say I look silly dancing around with ivy in
my hair?
Well yes, but so what?
Dionysos didn't specify his worshippers be young or
old—
he wants reverence from all.

Kadmos: You can't see this, Teiresias, but here's Pentheus
coming
and he has a wild look.
Wonder what's got into him.

[enter Pentheus]

Pentheus: I was out of the country but I kept hearing rumours
        of trouble in our city.
        Of women leaving home.
        Of fake Bakkhic revels deep in the mountains.
        Of women gone crazy for someone they call
            "Dionysos"
        whoever that is—
        they say "*daimon*" followed by a nervous hush.
        There's a lot of wine involved and creeping off into
            corners with men.
        Meanwhile they call themselves a prayer group!
        Obviously it's just sex. I've put most of them in jail.
        A few escaped—Agave,
        my own mother, for example, is still at large.
        I've got the police on it.
        Soon have them all locked up—
        put a stop to this Bakkhic nonsense.
        But people are talking about a certain Lydian stranger
            hanging around too.
        A sort of magician.
        Huckster.
        Swoony type,
        long hair, bedroom eyes, cheeks like wine.
        He mingles with the young girls night and day,
        claiming to show them some sort of *mystic thing*,
        claiming this Dionysos is a son of god
        and was sewn up in the thigh of Zeus—
        awful nonsense!
        The fact is
        he was burnt to bits along with his mother
        because she named Zeus as her paramour!

How about I investigate this guy (whoever he is)?
How about I curtail his *mystic thing*?

Oh my stars,
here's another wonder—Teiresias in fawnskins!
And you [laughs]—I'm sorry, grandfather, but you
     look like a lampshade.
Take off that ivy!
Was this your idea Teiresias?
Joining the Bakkhic bandwagon in hopes of a few
     extra commissions?
All that *daimonic* stuff is right up your alley, isn't it?
Lucky you're old and harmless or
I'd throw you in jail with the rest of them.
You pair of duffers,
don't you smell something off?
Women and wine—toxic combination!
Daimonic my foot!

Bakkhai: Might be a good idea,
if it's not too much bother,
to show more respect
for your old grandfather.
Not to mention the gods.

Teiresias: You're bold and loud and glib, Pentheus, you should
     have been a lawyer.
But you totally lack common sense.
This "new invented *daimon*" you laugh at—
take my word for it—
he's not one to laugh at.
He's going to be big.

Here's my view:
two things we mortals need to make life livable:
Demeter, on the one hand, grows all the food we eat
     on earth.
She is the dry element.
Dionysos, the wet element, gives us drink.
He showed us how to press liquor from grapes.
Wine is an escape from grief,
a slip into sleep,
a cool forgetting of the hot pains of day.
What better cure for being human?
And when we make libation to the gods we pour the
     god of wine himself—
it's how we pray.
Yet *this* is the divinity you want to laugh at?
Why?
Because of some legend that Zeus sewed him up in
     his thigh
with golden stitches?
I'll tell you what that means.
It's just a random homonym.
Zeus' *guilt* over his dalliance with Semele
was understood by simple minds
as *gilt*-edged stitches.
People do this kind of thing with stories all the
     time—
they hear what they want to hear.
It doesn't make the facts any less true.
The facts are,
this *daimon* is a prophet and you should by no means
     slight him.
Yes,

Bakkhic states of mind are laced with prophecy:
when the god enters your body you're suddenly
        speaking the future.
He plays a vital part in warfare too—that shock of fear
that runs right through an army before battle,
that shock is Dionysos.
Or that flash across the peaks of Delphi
tossing like a great wild spark from crag to crag
with a pine torch in each hand,
that's him.
But you,
Pentheus,
put too much emphasis on forcing your way:
do you really think
violence
is the only way to influence people?
Think again.
Accept this god.
Pour his wine, dance his dances, say yes!
Dionysos does not compel women to go mad for sex,
their own natures determine that.
Pure at heart is pure in life.
But admit this,
you love it when people throng your gates
and call your name.
He loves it too.
He wants respect, that's all.
So go ahead, ridicule Kadmos and me,
dressed up in our ivy
and tossing our old white heads.
We intend to dance for Dionysos, yes.
It's the right thing to do.

You must be out of your mind to go to war with a
    god like this.

Bakkhai: Good speech, old man, you've kept your Apollonian
        poise
and made the right noise
for Dionysos, an important god.

Kadmos: Teiresias gives good advice, my boy.
Come in with us, don't put yourself outside the law.
You're overexcited, your thoughts are all over the
        place.
But okay,
let's suppose for the moment this fellow is no god.
Why not say he is anyway?
It's a noble lie:
think what it does for the eminence of our family
to call Semele the mother of a god!
And don't forget your poor cousin Aktaion,
ripped apart by his own hunting dogs:
he prided himself he was better than Artemis at
        hunting.
Watch out for pride.
My dear boy, come in with us,
honour the god.
Here—
let me wreath your head in this bit of ivy—

Pentheus: Don't touch me!
Go play your Bakkhic burlesque somewhere else,
don't wipe it off on me.
And as for Professor Teiresias here,

29

your intellectual guide in this folly,
I'll see he gets his due.
[to his Guard]
Go
to Teiresias' little outpost
and bulldoze it.
Throw all his prophetic paraphenalia to the winds,
that will get him.
Then you [to another Guard] go
street to street through the town
and track down this girl-faced stranger.
Bring him to me.
His stink is
in our beds
and on our women.
I'll have him stoned to death—
bitter Theban aftertaste of his Dionysian dabbling!

Teiresias: Pentheus, I worry about you, I really do.
You were always hotheaded—
now you're sounding unhinged.
Kadmos, we better get going.
We should offer a special prayer to the god
on behalf of this man—
though he won't thank us—
and on behalf of the city of Thebes.
The god might do something radical otherwise.
Come on,
gather up your ivy.
We'll keep each other upright shall we?
Would be a bit embarrassing
to see the two old Bakkhai go tumbling in the dust

end over appetite!
But so be it.
Dionysos is god, our task is to serve him.
Just be careful of that grandson, Kadmos,
he'll bring remorse to your house.
I'm not speaking prophetically, these are facts.
One who speaks folly is a fool.

1st CHORAL ODE

Bakkhai:

Holiness
is a word I love to hear,
it sounds like wings to me,
wings brushing the world, grazing my life.
Pentheus has a harsh sound,
a negative sound.
He's a negative person.
He's against Dionysos,
against rejoicing,
against laughter,
against flutes—
not to mention the transcendent gladness of grapes and wine
so beneficial to body, soul and psyche's
interior design.

I'm saying
his tongue is unbridled,
his reasoning reckless,
his end may be hot and hard.
A life of quiet discretion,
still as a summer day,
holds a house together.
Cleverness is not wisdom.
Far off in the sky live the gods who never die
but they watch us.
They watch how far we press our limits:
there is a morning star,
there is an evening star,
don't press too far.

I dream of a perfectly clear afternoon
on the island where Aphrodite sits
counting her blessings
beside the erotic sea.
I dream of rivers
with a hundred mouths
and mountains
where the leaves turn over like silver fire.
Take me there, Dionysos!
O *daimon*!
O Bakkhos!
Take me
somewhere ruled by the law of desire
where we can dance you and dance you and never tire.

Our god loves festivity,
he loves serenity.
Whether you're high
or low
or rich
or simple,
all the same
Dionysos will fill your soul with peace.
It's not about intellectual prowess,
it's not about true and false,
it's pure release.
It's your life
night and day
free of grief:
Dionysos' gift.
Say no and he will hate you.
Choose this practice,

most people do—

I too.

[enter Guard]

Guard: Here we are, Pentheus, mission accomplished.
           And here's your quarry: we hunted him down.
           You called him a wild beast but we found him tame—
           didn't panic or run for it,
           didn't turn pale,
           just held out his hands—in fact
           he laughed,
           said "Okay tie me up!"
           and stood very patient while we put on the shackles.
           I was embarrassed.
           "Sorry, stranger" I said, "not my idea. Pentheus'
                orders."
           But here's something else—
           those Bakkhic women,
           the ones you arrested
           and locked up in jail—
           they've all gone free.
           Ran off to the mountains,
           skipping and dancing and calling the name of their god.
           The fetters simply fell off their feet,
           the doors swung open.
           By no human agency.
           This fellow has come to Thebes full of miracles,
                hasn't he?
           Well, it's your problem now.

Pentheus: Release his hands.
           He's in my net, he won't escape.
           Well,

stranger,
you're not bad-looking.
Obvious why you appeal to women—and that's
your main demographic in Thebes, am I right?
With that long flowing hair I can see you're no
    wrestler!
Indoor man, am I right?
Like to keep
your skin white,
out of the daylight,
soft to the touch—whose touch is it you dream of
in those long afternoons, those dim back bedrooms?
But no,
first,
who are you?
Where are you from?

Dionysos: That's easy. You've heard of the flowery hills of
        Tmolos I'm sure.

Pentheus: Yes I have. The hills around Sardis.

Dionysos: That's where I'm from. Lydia my homeland.

Pentheus: And what about this mystery religion of yours?
        Where's that from?

Dionysos: From Dionysos, son of Zeus.

Pentheus: You have some Zeus who plucks new gods out of the
        air?

Dionysos: The same Zeus who plucked one out of Semele, right
        here in Thebes.

Pentheus: Did he come to you as a dream in the night or in your
         waking hours?

Dionysos: My eyes were wide open. He teaches the mysteries
         personally.

Pentheus: What form do these mysteries take?

Dionysos: That's a secret. Not for the uninitiated.

Pentheus: And for the initiated, do they do some good?

Dionysos: You cannot know that. But it *is* worth knowing.

Pentheus: Aren't you a shrewd manager of data!
         Pricking my curiosity, am I right?

Dionysos: The mysteries are serious. They hate a trivializer.

Pentheus: You say you saw the god face to face. How did he
         look?

Dionysos: However he liked. I don't control that.

Pentheus: You're cagey, you keep deflecting my questions.

Dionysos: Good answers are wasted on a fool.

Pentheus: So are we the first place you've brought your new
         daimon?

Dionysos: Oh no, people are dancing for Dionysos pretty much
         everywhere else.

Pentheus: Foreigners all lack sense, compared to Greeks.

Dionysos: Well, there's more than one kind of sense. It's true
            they enjoy different customs.

Pentheus: And are your mysteries performed at night or in the day?

Dionysos: Mostly at night. Darkness is serious.

Pentheus: Yes it is, seriously corrupting, for women.

Dionysos: Can't corruption be found in daylight too?

Pentheus: Oh stop being clever! There's a penalty for that!

Dionysos: Stop being superficial. You slight the god.

Pentheus: I can't believe your arrogance, you casuistical Bakkhic
            little show-off!

Dionysos: And there's a penalty for that? What? *Scare me*.

Pentheus: First thing would be a crewcut.

Dionysos: But my hair is holy, I grew it for the god.

Pentheus: And hand over that stupid thyrsos.

Dionysos: Take it yourself. It belongs to Dionysos.

Pentheus: Then I'll put you in jail.

Dionysos: The god will let me out.

Pentheus: Sure, whenever you call him I suppose.

Dionysos: He's already here now.

Pentheus: Where? I don't see any god.

Dionysos: Right where I am. You don't see because you aren't
            serious.

Pentheus [to Guards]:   Seize this man! He mocks me! He mocks
            Thebes!

Dionysos: I warn you, don't do it.

Pentheus: I'm the one who gives the orders here.

Dionysos: You don't know what your life is, nor what you're
            doing, nor who you are.

Pentheus: I am Pentheus, son of Agave, son of Echion!

Dionysos: That is the saddest name I've ever heard.

Pentheus [to Guard]:   Go.
            Lock him up in the stables—
            he can commune with the serious darkness in there.
            Teach the horses to dance.
            And these women of his,
            these cymbal-bangers and drum-thumpers,
            we'll sell into slavery or put to work at our looms.

Dionysos: I'm going.
            But you cannot make me suffer what I'm not destined
            to suffer.

> And for your insults
> you will have to answer to Dionysos,
> whom you say does not exist.
> In imprisoning us you wrong *him*.

[exeunt Dionysos, Pentheus and Guard into palace]

2nd CHORAL ODE

Bakkhai:

O Dirke,
river of Thebes,
lady river,
virgin river,
daughter of Acheloos the river,
once upon a time
you welcomed to your waters
the infant Dionysos
when Zeus translated him from fire
into his own thigh
and gave him to Thebes
as
Bakkhos
born of a masculine womb.
So why do you repudiate me now?
Why do you turn away
from my dances?
One day yet,
by the clustering grace of the vine,
by the glowing green delirium of the vine,
by the joyous blue blush of the vine,
I swear
you will come to care
passionately
for the god we call
Bakkhos,
Twiceborn,
Dithyrambos,
Bromios,

Euios,
Dionysos!

Such anger,
such anger
he shows,
that earthborn snakebegotten Pentheus,
son of Echion, a monster without a face.
This is no human entity,
he comes from giants and blood.
He pits himself against gods.
And soon he will have me in his prison—
I who belong to Bromios!
Already my comrade
is locked up in the dark.
Do you see this, Dionysos?
Do you see
how
passionately
your prophets struggle?
Lord,
come down from Olympos,
shake your thyrsos
and crush
the *hybris*
of this wrongminded man!

O

Dionysos,
where are you?
Roving the mountains?
Lost in a dreamy afternoon

on Mount Olympos
where Orpheus
once
taught the trees to walk
and the animals to dance to his tune?
O blessed Pieria,
Dionysos reveres you.
Dionysos is coming,
he is not far to seek.
Leading his Bakkhai
river by river,
he will cross the Axios,
a speedy river,
he will cross the Lydias,
a river whose waters
(so I have heard)
make the ground rich and the horses sleek.

Dionysos [from offstage]: *IO!* Hear me! Hear my voice!
          O Bakkhai! O Bakkhai!

Bakkhai: Who is this? Where does this Dionysos-voice come
          from?

Dionysos: *IO!* I call again,
          I, son of Semele, son of Zeus.

Bakkhai: *IO* master! Master come to us! Bromios! Bromios!

Dionysos: Spirit of earthquake, shake the floor of the world!

Bakkhai: *A! A!* Soon Pentheus' house will be broken apart!
          The god is all through the house.

Worship him!
Yes! But oh—
look the stones are sliding off the roof!
Listen,
Dionysos lifts his cry inside the house—

Dionysos: Light this blaze! Make Pentheus' house a conflagration!

Bakkhai: *A! A!* See that fire?
Those flames surrounding Semele's tomb?
Throw yourselves to the ground, Bakkhai!
Our king is turning the house upside down—

[enter Dionysos]

Dionysos: Okay ladies, up we get,
no more crouching,
no more sobbing.
I guess you saw Bakkhos topple Pentheus' house?

Bakkhai: O wild great light of your voice, is it you?
What joy to see you! I was so lonely!

Dionysos: You lost heart
when you saw me go into the big dark interior?

Bakkhai: Of course I did! You are my only shelter.
How did you escape?

Dionysos: Easily.

Bakkhai: But he tied your hands with ropes.

43

Dionysos: Just between you and me,
            I had a bit of fun with him and his ropes.
            He thought he tied me up you see, but he hadn't laid
                 a hand on me—
            he got hold of a bull that was stabled there,
            poor creature trying to eat its dinner.
            That's where the ropes went,
            he wrapped that bull from stem to stern—
            hard work! he was panting and sweating and biting
                 his lip.
            I sat by and watched quietly.
            It was just then Bakkhos shook the house
            and sent up a flame on Semele's tomb.
            Pentheus panicked,
            fancied his house was on fire,
            started running back and forth shouting orders
            about buckets and water,
            put every servant to work,
            total waste of time.
            Then it suddenly struck him I might escape.
            He dropped his bucket,
            grabbed a sword
            and raced inside.
            Where,
            as it seems to me,
            but this is just one man's opinion,
            Bromios fashioned a simulacrum of me.
            Pentheus leapt upon it, stabbing the air,
            slaughtering me.
            Then Bromios added injury to insult—
            he did bring down the house!
            Dashed it.

Smashed it.
Disarticulated it.
To bits.
So much for trying to put me in jail.
The great warrior sank to the ground exhausted.
Man against god: never works.
I made my exit peacefully.
No idea what Pentheus is up to now.
Oh, here comes someone, I bet it's him.
What will he say? I wonder.
No matter how hot he blows,
I'll be my
simple
smiling
self.
A wise man is a well-tempered man.

[enter Pentheus]

Pentheus: Ghastly day. That stranger escaped me!
though I secured him with stout ropes.
Here's the man! What's going on?
How did you get yourself out here?!

Dionysos: Take a breath, Pentheus.
In through the nose, out through the mouth.

Pentheus: What about the ropes, the knots?
I tied you up myself!

Dionysos: I believe I mentioned someone would release me?

Pentheus: Someone like who? You're always trying to sound so
             mysterious.

Dionysos: The one who bestows grapes and vines and wines on
             humankind.

Pentheus: Ah yes, that welcome contribution to society.

Dionysos: You don't approve?

Pentheus: Lock the doors! Bar the gates! Close the city down!

Dionysos: Why bother? Doors don't stop gods.

Pentheus: Oh stop being so *wise*. Where does it get you?

Dionysos: Can't do it, wisdom is my nature.
             Where does it get me? Well, we'll see.
             But here comes a man you should listen to.
             He's down from the mountains with special news.
             I'll wait.

[enter Herdsman]

Herdsman: Pentheus, king of Thebes,
             I've come from Mt Kithairon
             where the peaks are always white with snow.

Pentheus: Important news?

Herdsman: Those Bakkhai, those hysterical women, I've seen them!
             The ones who went flying from their houses barefoot!

I need to tell you the strange things they're doing—
    beyond strange!
Can I speak freely?
I'm nervous of your quick temper, sir,
your kingly sensitivity.

Pentheus: Say what you like, you're safe.
It wouldn't be decent to blame a law-abiding man,
    would it.
But the stranger your report of Bakkhic doings,
the more I'll punish that fellow
who indoctrinated them
into this whole dubious Dionysian business.

Herdsman: Well, so
we're driving our cattle uphill to pasture,
it was just at sunrise,
when I see three groups of those women—
three circles—
one with Autonoe,
another surrounding Agave your mother,
a third with Ino.
Lying fast asleep.
They were all so *still*.
Some had leaned their backs against the pine trees,
some had pillows made of piles of leaves.
Calm as buttons on a shirt.
You told us to look out for drunkenness,
wild music,
wantoning through the woods—
there was none of that.
But you know, cattle are noisy, shuffling and mooing,

your mother starts awake, yells that yell of hers
to rouse the Bakkhai
and they spring straight up,
rubbing the sleep from their eyes
yet somehow instantly organized—I was impressed.
Young women, old ones, girls unwed,
they shook out their hair and fastened their fawnskins,
with snakes that slid up to lick their cheeks,
some (new mothers who'd left their babies at home)
cradled wolf cubs or deer in their arms and suckled
        them,
others were wreathing their heads with ivy and oak
        and bryony.
One took a thyrsos and struck a rock. Clear water
        gushed out.
Another pierced the ground to make wine flow—gift
        of a god—
and those who desired it scratched the earth and got
        white milk,
while from many a thyrsos
sweet honey was dripping.
If you'd been there,
if you'd seen what I saw,
you'd be offering prayers to this god you denounce.
So we gathered together,
we cowherds and shepherds,
to discuss these bizarre goings-on
and up gets one of the drovers who knew how to talk.
You mountain men (he addresses us)
how about we go hunt down Agave?
Pluck Pentheus' mother from her Bakkhic revels
and do a favour for the king?
It seemed a good idea.

We set ourselves in ambush there in the thickets
and at a certain moment the women began to whirl
and stamp
and call out *Iakkhos! Bromios! Son of Zeus!*
until the entire mountain streamed with sound
and every animal was racing—
no part of the place was not in motion.
And as it happened Agave came swerving past me—
I leapt at her,
she screamed
O my running dogs! O my swift hounds!
men are hunting us down!
Follow me now!
That thyrsos in your hand
is a weapon,
use it!
We fled.
They would have torn us limb from limb.
They did attack our herds: you could have seen
a woman pull a calf to pieces as it bellowed alive in
her bare hands!
Others were ripping apart full-grown heifers—
there were ribs and hooves scattered up and down,
chunks of flesh dripped from the pine trees, blood
everywhere.
Proud angry bulls stumbled to the ground under the
hands of girls
who clawed the meat off them
quicker than you could wink your royal eye.
Then all of a sudden they took off like a flock of birds
to the fields below, along the river, beneath Kithairon.
Two villages there.
The women fell on them like a ransacking army,

tore the place to shreds,
stole the children from the houses,
and carried off all the plunder they could pile on their
    shoulders
without dropping a thing.

And you know, their hair was on fire yet it didn't burn.

Now the villagers got angry.
And here was a sight right terrible to see.
For their sharpened weapons drew no blood at all
while those of the women—!
You know a thyrsos can make quite a wound.
So the men fled.
Some god engineered the whole thing, is my guess.
Anyway, the women went back up the hill where
    they started,
to fountains made by their god.
They washed their hands
and let the snakes
lick the blood from their cheeks.
Whoever this *daimon* is, sir, welcome him to Thebes.
People say he is important.
Extremely important.
They say he gave the gift of wine to men:
why, without wine we've no freedom from pain.
Without wine there's no sex.
Without sex
life isn't worth living.

[exit Herdsman]

Bakkhai: I fear speaking freely to the king.
           Still, it must be said.
           Dionysos is inferior *to no god*.

Pentheus: This Bakkhic insanity is catching like wildfire.
           What a disgrace! People watch us and laugh.
           It's no time to shrink back—
           go to the gates of the city.
           Call out every man who can carry a shield,
           ride a horse,
           hurl a spear
           or fit an arrow to the bowstring:
           we're going to make war on the Bakkhai.
           It is beyond endurance—to suffer all this at the hands
                 of women!

Dionysos: You're the type of person who listens
           yet you do not hear.
           You've used me badly
           yet I warn you,
           don't take up arms against a god.
           Stay quiet.
           Bromios will not endure you driving the Bakkhai
                 from his mountain.

Pentheus: Don't lecture me!
           You escaped prison, be happy with that.
           Or shall I throw you back in jail?

Dionysos: I'd offer worship to this god,
           rather than rage at him, mortal against god.

Pentheus: Worship, good idea! I'll worship a big bloody pile of
            Bakkhic women!

Dionysos: No, in fact they'll make you turn and run,
            these women with their homemade weapons,
            they will shame you.

Pentheus: Oh why am I entangled in this hopeless conversation?
            The fellow never stops talking!

Dionysos: Oh come on, there's still a way to make things right.

Pentheus: How? Submit to my inferiors?

Dionysos: I'll bring the women here myself. No weapons.

Pentheus: This is some trick, some plan, some stratagem.
            I don't trust you.

Dionysos: Why not? My plan is simply to save you.

Pentheus: You've dreamed this up in collaboration with those
                women—
            so they can keep carousing forever.

Dionysos: Well, in collaboration with a god anyway.

Pentheus: Bring me my sword! I'll make you stop talking!

Dionysos: Aah.
            Then how about this. Would you like to see
            what the women are up to on that mountain?

Pentheus: Oh I'd give anything for that.

Dionysos: You're suddenly avid. Can you say why?

Pentheus: Of course it would pain me to see women crazy with
            drink.

Dionysos: But a pain mixed with pleasure perhaps.

Pentheus: Exactly. I can sit quiet by a pine tree.

Dionysos: Hiding? But if you hide they'll smell you out.

Pentheus: Good point. I'll stay in the open.

Dionysos: Then let's go. Are you ready?

Pentheus: Ready! Don't waste any more time!

Dionysos: First you must put on women's clothes.

Pentheus: Why? Change myself to a woman?

Dionysos: If they see a man there, you're dead.

Pentheus: Another good point. You're sharp.

Dionysos: Dionysos taught me everything I know.

Pentheus: So how do we go about this?

Dionysos: I'll come into the house and dress you myself.

Pentheus: Dress me as a woman? I'm too embarrassed!

Dionysos: Lost your appetite? No more spying on maenads?

Pentheus: What kind of women's dress did you have in mind?

Dionysos: Well, first I'll give you long flowing hair.

Pentheus: Then what? Jewellery?

Dionysos: Then a dress to your ankles. And a binding for your hair.

Pentheus: Anything else?

Dionysos: A thyrsos of course. And a fawnskin.

Pentheus: No, I can't do it. Dress as a woman. No.

Dionysos: Well, if you simply
              march up the mountain and make war on them,
              you'll cause a blood bath.

Pentheus: True. I need to reconnoitre first.

Dionysos: Now you're thinking. No point hunting trouble with
                    trouble, is there?

Pentheus: But how shall I get through town unseen?

Dionysos: I know a back way.

Pentheus: The important thing is, those women must not laugh
                    at me.
              Let's go inside, I'll decide what to do

Dionysos: Fine. I'm ready, whatever you choose.

Pentheus: Either make war on them or listen to you.

[exit Pentheus into palace]

Dionysos: Ladies, the man is in the net!
            He's on his way to the Bakkhai,
            he'll pay the ultimate price.
            Dionysos, the rest is up to you.
            You're close to us now,
            you're very close.
            It's time to punish Pentheus: first
            craze his brain,
            send a scamper of madness into it—
            otherwise he'll never put on women's clothes.
            And
            given the way he threatened me,
            I'd like to see him made mock of,
            paraded through town in all his ridiculous female
                  finery.
            So
            I'll go rig him up, put on his dress—he'll
            wear that dress to Hades
            after his mother slaughters him with her own hands.
            And he will come *to know Dionysos,*
            son of Zeus,
            true and consummate god,
            god of the intensities of terror,
            god of the gentlest human peace.

3rd CHORAL ODE

Bakkhai:
When shall I
set my white foot
in the allnight dances,
when shall I
lift my throat
to the dewy air,

like a fawn
skylarking
in the
green joy of the meadow—
she runs
free
from the hunt and the hunter,
she leaps
over the net
as he cries up his dogs,
with storms
in her feet
she
sprints
the plain,
races
the river
flies
down
to the shadows that deepen the trees,
overjoyed!
at the sheer absence of men.
What is wisdom?

                                    What feels better
             than to hold your hand over the head of your enemy?
                                                Who
                                               does
                                                not
                                               love
                                               this
                                            feeling?

It moves
    so slowly
            – the force of the gods—
yet it is absolutely guaranteed
to arrive.
To punish
    human folly
            and the arrogance
                    of a private theology.
                    Ingenious
            how a god can hide
            and then

leap out

            on the unholy man.
            To think or act outside the law is never right.
            But this is valid—
            this thing we call the *daimonic*
                        ancient,
                    elemental,
        fixed in law and custom,
    grown out of nature itself.

                                    What is wisdom?
                                    What feels better

than to bring your hand down on the head of your enemy?
Who
does
not
love
this
feeling?

Happy is he who escapes the winter sea,
finds a harbour,
prevails over pain.
Still, one man will always outdo another in wealth or power.
And hopes
are countless, they come on like waves,
rising
and
falling.
Just be happy,
day to day:
this I call blessed.

[enter Dionysos]

Dionysos: You! Pentheus! I'm talking to you!
              Still so keen on seeing sights you should not see?
              Still hungry for mischief?
              Come out and show me your Bakkhic get-up,
              your maenad-suit,
              your costume for spying on women.

[enter Pentheus]

              You look like one of Kadmos' daughters!

Pentheus: You know, I seem to see two suns.
             And a double Thebes, each with all its seven gates.
             And you look like a bull leading me in procession—
             you've got horns growing out your head!
             Were you perhaps an animal all the time?
             You're certainly a bull at the moment.

Dionysos: The god is with us now.
             He's come round, he's on our side.
             You're seeing as you ought to see.

Pentheus: How do I look?
             Is this the way Ino stands?
             Or Agave my mother?

Dionysos: I feel I'm seeing them in person.
             But here, this bit of hair is out of place—
             I had it tucked under, did I not?

Pentheus: I was tossing my head back and forth like a maenad
                   inside the house.

Dionysos: I'll redo it—I'm here to serve you. Hold still.

Pentheus: Oh lovely. You redo it. I'm in your hands.

Dionysos: And your belt is loose, your pleats uneven,
             the hem's slipping down around your ankles.

Pentheus: Is it? Possibly, on the right anyway.
             Over here it hangs straight, so far as I can see.

Dionysos: You'll think me your best friend I'm sure,
            when you see how sober and sensible the Bakkhai are,
            not what you expect.

Pentheus: Do I take the thyrsos in my right hand
            or like this,
            to look really Bakkhic?

Dionysos: Right hand.
            Raise it in time with your right foot.
            I'm so glad you had a change of heart!

Pentheus: I'll be able to lift Mt Kithairon on my bare shoulders,
            Bakkhic women and all, am I right?

Dionysos: No problem. Your whole attitude before was unsound
            but not anymore!

Pentheus: Should we take crowbars?
            Or shall I just put my shoulder under the mountain
                    and shove?

Dionysos: Be careful though, you musn't do damage to the
                    temples of the Nymphs
            or the places where Pan plays his pipes.

Pentheus: Good point. Brute force is out. Doesn't work with
                    women anyhow.
            I'll hide in the pines.

Dionysos: You'll hide in the hiding place a man should have
            who comes to spy on the Bakkhai.

Pentheus: You know, I can see them in my mind's eye,
            little birds in the bracken,
            all tangled up in sex.

Dionysos: Well that's your mission, right?
            Catch them at it!
            Unless you're caught first.

Pentheus: Take me right through the middle of the city:
            I'm the only man bold enough to do this.

Dionysos: Yes, you alone bear this burden on behalf of Thebes.
            A contest awaits you: the contest of your destiny.
            Follow me.
            I am your guide and saviour.
            Someone else will bring you home.

Pentheus: My mother!

Dionysos: You'll be conspicuous to all.

Pentheus: That's my hope.

Dionysos: You'll be carried aloft.

Pentheus: What a luxury!

Dionysos: In the arms of your mother.

Pentheus: Now you're spoiling me!

Dionysos: Indeed I am.

Pentheus: But I deserve it.

Dionysos: You are an amazing strange man
            and amazing strange experiences await you.
            Your celebrity will reach high heaven.
            Open your arms, Agave,
            open your arms, daughters of Kadmos!
            I am leading this young man to a great contest, to his
                 ultimate performance.
            And who will win?
            I will win.
            Bromios and I.
            As for the rest: soon enough obvious.

[exit Pentheus]

4th CHORAL ODE

Bakkhai:

Run, you dogs of madness!

Run to the mountain

where the daughters of Kadmos

are dancing!

Sting them and drive them

to hunt down that man—

dressed up as a woman

he spies on women—

his eye has a crazy glow.

First

his mother will spot him

ducking and dodging,

hopping and hiding,

sneaking and sniffing

from cliff to crag

and

she will call out to her maenads:

Who is this man

come to our mountain

to hunt us from peak to peak,

O Bakkhai?

Who gave him birth?

Surely no woman!

His mother must be some lion, some Gorgon!

Into the throat

of

the

ungodly

                    unlawful
                  unrighteous
                    earthborn
                       son
                    of Echion
                   let justice
                 sink her sword
                        !

His judgment is wrong,
        his anger chaotic,
              his arrogance out of control.
                    He dispatches himself against you,
                    Bakkhos,
                    against your mother,
                    against your holy rites.
                    He is a violent man.
                              But
                              Death will discipline him.
                              Death takes no excuses.
                    To accept that we are mortal
helps us live without pain.
                    Myself,
                    I've no interest in wisdom.
                    I hunt another quarry,
                    by day,
                    by night:
        the great clear joy of living pure and reverently,
                    rejecting injustice
                    and honouring gods.

                    Into the throat
                       of

                    the
                  ungodly
                  unlawful
                 unrighteous
                  earthborn
                    son
                  of Echion
                 let justice
               sink her sword
                    !

                         Show yourself, Bakkhos!
                                  Be a bull,
                          be a snake,
                        be a lion,
                       be manifest!
                  Come with your little net
                 and your fatal smile,
              your little smile
             and your fatal net,
        hunt down the hunter!
        Trip him and tangle him!
        Let him fall under a pack of maenads!

[enter Servant]

Servant: This house was fortunate once.
            Founded by Kadmos,
            who sowed an earthborn crop from dragon's seed.
            How I grieve for you, though I am but a slave,
            still I grieve for you.

Bakkhai: What is it? News of the Bakkhai?

Servant: Pentheus is dead, the son of Echion.

Bakkhai: O Bromios!
              You are revealed to eye, mind and judgment a great god!

Servant: I beg your pardon? What are you saying?
              You women rejoice at my master's downfall?

Bakkhai: We are foreign, we sing a foreign song of joy.
              No more cowering! No more prison!

Servant: You think Thebes has no men left to govern you?

Bakkhai: Dionysos, not Thebes, is my government.

Servant: Understood, ladies, but to gloat over others' misfortune
              is not decent.

Bakkhai: How did he die? I want to know details.
              He was an unjust man.
              A thoroughly unjust man.

Servant: We had left behind the outskirts of Thebes and the
                      river Asopos,
              heading for Mt Kithairon—it was Pentheus in front,
              me following,
              and a stranger who offered to act as our guide.
              We came to a grassy glen,
              walking silently,
              looking to see and not be seen.
              There was a hollow between two hills,
              crossed by streams and shaded by pine trees

where the maenads were sitting happily working at
     little tasks.
Some were rewinding a thyrsos with tendrils of ivy,
others frisking like colts set free
and singing Bakkhic songs back and forth.
But Pentheus, the hapless man, couldn't quite see the
     women
and said to our guide,
"From where I stand I can't make out those imposters,
those maenads,
but up on the bank,
if I were to climb a tall pine,
I could get a good view of all their obscene goings-on."

And then I saw the stranger work a miracle.

Seizing the top branch of a towering pine
he brought it down,
down,
down
to the black ground
curved taut like a bow
or a rim forced round a wheel.
So did the stranger force that pine tree down to
     earth—
no mortal could have done it.
Then he sat Pentheus upon the branch
and let the tree go straight up through his hands,
gradually, gently,
lest it unseat the rider.
And up the tree rose to the sky—
straight up—with my master crouched on top.

And now the maenads saw him more than he saw
        them,
still he was not completely visible on his perch.
But the stranger suddenly vanished
and a voice came out of the air—
it was probably Dionysos—shouting:
"Here he is, women! I bring you the man
who mocks me and mocks my holy rites.
Punish him!"
And as he said this
a column of fire shot between heaven and earth. Then
        silence fell.
Silence through the wood and on the leaves and every
        animal was silent.
You could hear not a twitch.
The Bakkhai got to their feet and were peering
        around—
they hadn't clearly recognized the voice.
Again it rang out.
And now they knew his cry!
Off they shot with the speed of doves—
Agave, her sisters, all the Bakkhai—
racing over glen and stream and jagged rock,
maddened by the breath of god.
And when they saw my master sitting atop a pine tree
they climbed a facing hill and began pelting him with
        rocks,
they hurled pine boughs like javelins,
or used the thyrsos as a spear.
Yet they kept missing.
Poor Pentheus was out of range, although absolutely
        helpless.
Finally they started ripping off branches of oak

to use as crowbars
and uproot the tree.
It didn't work.
Agave spoke:
"Come, maenads, stand round in a circle
and grip the trunk of the tree.
Up there's a wild animal we must capture
or he'll broadcast the secrets of our god!"
With that,
countless hands took hold of the pine tree and tore it
	from the ground.
And
down,
down,
down
he fell
to the ground
from his high seat,
yelping and sobbing.

Pentheus.
He was close to understanding his own doom.
Agave,
as priestess of the slaughter
launched herself first upon him.
He pulled the headdress from his head
in hopes that she,
his poor luckless mother,
would know him, would spare him—
he touched her cheek and cried out,
"Mother, it's me! I am the child you bore in the house
	of Echion!
Pity me, mother,

do not murder your own child, whatever his
     mistakes!"
But she
was foaming at the mouth,
was rolling back her eyes,
was out of her mind.
Bakkhos had possessed her,
she did not even hear the boy.
Seizing his left arm by the wrist
she planted her foot against his ribs
and ripped the arm off at the shoulder—
not by her own strength, the god made it easy.
Meanwhile Ino was working away at the other side
stripping the meat from the bone,
and Autonoe with the whole mob of Bakkhai
attacked.
It was one float of hideous sound—
him gasping and groaning,
them shrieking their war cry.
One carried off an arm, another a foot still in its shoe,
his ribs were laid bare of flesh
and every woman
drenched in blood
for they were playing ball with his body parts.

So the corpse was lying all over the place,
some by the rocks, some in the woods,
hard to find.
But the head,
the terrible head,
his mother picks up
and (as if it were some mountain lion's)
impales on top of her thyrsos!
And she's carrying it now,

70

marching right down Kithairon,
leaving her sisters behind—
yes, she's on her way here.
Exulting in that dark and bloody prize
and calling out—
                    "Bakkhos,
                        my partner in the hunt!
                    my comrade in the victory!
O what a victory!"

But the trophy in her hands is her own tears.

Anyway, I'll get out of here before she arrives.
To live and think and act within measure,
reverencing the gods,
this is a man's finest possession.

[exit Servant]

Bakkhai:

                We dance for Bakkhos,
                    we dance for death!
                    Pentheus'
                    death—
                    born of a snake,
                    dressed as a woman,
he took up a thyrsos and followed a bull directly down to Hades.
                For the thyrsos is certain death!
                    You Bakkhai,
                    you women of Thebes,
                your beautiful victory finishes in tears,
                your glorious game ends in lamentation,
                    your lovely hand streams with blood
                        as it lifts your own son!

But look, I see Agave running towards us,
       her eyes are insane.
    Give her a wild welcome,
      a Bakkhic welcome!

[enter Agave carrying the head of Pentheus]

Agave: O Bakkhai!
             O women of Asia!

Bakkhai: Why are you shouting?

Agave: We bring from the mountains
           a newcut tendril,
              a lovely bit of hunting.

Bakkhai: I see.
                      And I welcome you,
                      dear comrade.

Agave: I caught him myself with my bare hands—
                     cub of a wild mountain lion, look!

Bakkhai: Mountain? What mountain

Agave: Kithairon—

Bakkhai: Kithairon?

Agave: —slaughtered him!

Bakkhai: Who struck the blow?

Agave: Me! My prize!
                                          "Agave the blessed"
          is what they call me!

Bakkhai: Who else was there?

Agave: Kadmos'—

Bakkhai: Kadmos?

Agave: Kadmos' daughters
                                  came upon the animal after me.
                                  Lucky hunting!

Bakkhai: Lucky indeed.

Agave: Won't you share my feast?

Bakkhai: Share it?
          O my dear.
          O pity!

Agave: What a fresh bloom he is,
                                  just a kid, just a calf—
                                  here, see the down on his cheek,
                                  the long soft hair.

Bakkhai: That long hair
          does give him an animal look.

Agave: Our Bakkhos is wise,
                                  is he not,
                                  a wise hunter.

How wisely
he drove the maenads upon this beast!

Bakkhai: Oh yes he's a hunter.

Agave: Do you praise me?

Bakkhai: Oh yes I praise you.

Agave: And soon the men of Thebes—

Bakkhai: not to say Pentheus your son—

Agave: —will praise his mother
who caught this wild thing,
this lion cub.

Bakkhai: Extraordinary catch!

Agave: Extraordinary experience.

Bakkhai: So you're happy?

Agave: I'm overjoyed.
It was magnificent—
the day, the hunt, the spectacle—
magnificent!

Bakkhai: Show your prize to the people, then,
show your catch, poor woman.

Agave: O citizens of beautifully-towered Thebes,
come see my catch!

We daughters of Kadmos hunted and caught
this wild animal,
not with javelins,
not with nets,
just the slender fingers of our own white hands!
What are they worth now,
your boasts, your useless weaponry?
We took this beast barehanded!
We tore it limb from limb!
Where's my father, where's the old man?
Let him approach.
And Pentheus my son, where's he?
I want him to set up a ladder against the house
and nail this head to the roofbeam:
my trophy.
My lion.
I won it myself.

[enter Kadmos with servants and body of Pentheus]

Kadmos: Follow me, servants.
            Bring the thing here.
            The thing that was Pentheus.
            Bring it in front of the house.
            I had to search for this body all over Kithairon.
            On the rocks, in the woods, the parts were scattered,
                  lost.
            I found them. I made a pile. It was hard to do that.
            Why did I go up there?
            Because I heard of my daughters' monstrous acts.
            I had already returned to town with Teiresias
            but
            I went back to the mountain,

75

I carried my child away.
Maenads killed him.
I saw Ino and Autonoe up there,
still ecstatic,
raving in the oak trees:
oh it was pitiful.
And then someone told me
of Agave on her way down to Thebes,
dancing, delirious.
And they were right.
I'm looking at her now.
It's no pretty sight.

Agave: Father,
now you can boast you have the best daughters in the
            world!
I mean all of us, but especially me.
I left my loom and weaving to go after bigger game—
to hunt wild beasts with my bare hands!
I've got one here—look! I brought this trophy for
            your house.
Take it, father.
You can hang it up!
Invite your friends, throw a banquet, show off my
            prowess!
Because you know you are a blessed man,
                    a blessed man, father!
                        What a family of achievers we are!

Kadmos: O grief without measure.
I don't know how to look at you.
Your poor butchering hands.
What a first-rate sacrifice you offer the gods!

What a banquet you have in mind!
And you wish to invite all of Thebes? You're inviting
     me too?
O sorrow.
Your sorrow.
My sorrow.
Certainly, yes,
he treats us with justice but
       the god goes too far—
          Bromios: our destroyer!
          Bromios: our family!

Agave: Well aren't you grumpy! Old age is like that, always
     scowling.
I wish my son were more like me—lucky in the hunt
when he goes out after game with the young men of
     Thebes.
But all he cares about is making war on gods.
He needs a bit of a talking-to from you, father,
Will someone call him out here
so he can witness my good fortune?

Kadmos: [*PHEU PHEU*] O pity.
If you see what you've done the pain will fall.
Stay in this ignorance forever
and you'll be unhappy
but you won't know it.

Agave: What do you mean unhappy? Is something wrong?

Kadmos: First, look up. Look at the sky.

Agave: Okay. Why?

Kadmos: Does it look normal? Or is it changing?

Agave: It's brighter than before, sort of glowing.

Kadmos: And that fluttering inside you, you still feel that?

Agave: I don't know, I'm not sure.
           I'm coming back into my own mind somehow,
           my thoughts are moving, shifting, breaking up.

Kadmos: Can you hear me? Can you answer plainly?

Agave: I've forgotten what we were talking about.

Kadmos: Whose house did you go to when you married?

Agave: Echion's. You gave me to Echion.
           One of the Sown Men, as they say.

Kadmos: What child did you bear to your husband there?

Agave: Pentheus.

Kadmos: And whose head is that you have in your hands?

Agave: A lion's head. So the hunters told me.

Kadmos: Look at it now. Just take a moment. Look straight.

Agave: [EA] What am I seeing? What is this I have in my
               hands?

Kadmos: Look. Understand.

Agave: I see unimaginable pain.

Kadmos: Does it look like the head of a lion now?

Agave: No. I'm holding the head of Pentheus.

Kadmos: Mourned by me before you knew who he was.

Agave: Who killed him? How did he come to my hands?

Kadmos: Truth is an unbearable thing. And its timing is bad.

Agave: Tell me, my heart is leaping out of me.

Kadmos: You killed him, you and your sisters.

Agave: Where? In the house? Some other place?

Kadmos: Where the dogs tore Aktaion apart long ago.

Agave: Why did the poor boy go to Mt Kithairon?

Kadmos: He went to mock the god and your Bakkhic rituals.

Agave: Me—what was I doing up there?

Kadmos: Raving, mad. The whole city went mad for Bakkhos.

Agave: Dionysos destroyed us. I recognize it now.

Kadmos: He was outraged by your *hybris*. You denied he was a
            god.

Agave: Where is the dear body of my son, father?

Kadmos: I gathered the pieces myself.
            It wasn't easy.
            Here.

Agave: You've fitted the limbs together so it looks decent?

Kadmos: See for yourself.

Agave: Ah.
            His body.
            His dear, dear body.
            This is my son.
            This is what I did.
            Come, old man, let us place the head and cover him
            and lay him properly in the grave.
            He deserves that.
            For I do not believe my son had any share in my folly.

Kadmos: But he *was* like you, he denied the god.
            And so has joined us all together in a single
                ruination—
            you, himself, our house and me.
            I never had sons myself
            and now I see
            the fruit of your womb, woman,
            dying the worst death possible
            right before my eyes.

You were the light of our house, child,
as son of my daughter, you held it together.
And what a terror to the city—no one dared insult me
once they saw your face,
you'd make them pay!
But now I'll be an exile, driven from home and from
     honour,
Kadmos, the great,
who sowed the Theban race
and reaped fair harvest.
O beloved one—
I know you are dead but still, child, still,
you count
as my most beloved –
never again will you touch my face
or fold me to you saying,
"Does someone slight you, old man?
Does someone disrespect or vex or make you sad?
Tell me, I'll punish him!"
No.
I am brokenhearted now
and you are lost to us,
your mother ruined,
her sisters bereft.
If anyone here despises the *daimonic,*
let him look on this boy's death and believe in gods.

Bakkhai: I feel your sorrow, Kadmos.
           Your grandson's punishment was justified,
           yet agony for you.

Agave: O father! Here is my life turned upside down!

[enter Dionysos]

Dionysos: I am the god triumphant.
                You squandered all your chance to worship me.
                That was unwise.
                You must leave this city and go among strangers.
                You are defiled.
                And you insulted me—
                you claimed I was a mortal man.
                Now learn,
                murderous woman,
                learn what kind of god I am.
                You will turn into a serpent,
                your wife into a savage snake.
                You and she,
                as the oracle foretells,
                will lead a barbarian army
                in the sacking of cities
                and the laying waste of shrines,
                then journey miserably home.
                But Ares will save you,
                and translate you alive to the land of the blessed.
                I say these things,
                not as the child of a mortal father,
                but as son of Zeus.
                Had you known how to live within measure,
                you'd be prospering now,
                and the son of Zeus your ally.

Kadmos: Dionysos, hear our prayer. We did wrong.

Dionysos: You've learned too late. Far too late.

Kadmos: Yes. Yes. But your retaliation is *too much*.

Dionysos: I am a god and you insulted me!

Kadmos: Gods should not resemble humans in their anger.

Dionysos: My father Zeus approved all this a long time ago.

Agave: It is decided, old man. Alas!
            We go into exile. Into despair.

Dionysos: Exactly.
            Why then delay?

[exit Dionysos]

Kadmos: O my child.
            Evil, evil, is where we are,
            you and your sisters and I,
            this is the worst.
            I'm to make my way as a stranger in strange lands.
            I'm to live as a snake!
            I'm to lead an army
            against the altars and tombs of the Greeks.
            I will find no release from my misery,
            not even by sailing down the river of death to peace-
                ful oblivion.

Agave: O father!
            I'll go into exile, I'll never see you again!

Kadmos: Why wrap your arms around me, you poor child,
            like a young swan with its whiteheaded father?

Agave:	Where shall I go? I have no home!
Kadmos:	Child, I don't know. Your old father is not much help.
Agave:	Farewell, my house, farewell my city. I am leaving you now for the absolute pain of exile.
Kadmos:	Go.
Agave:	I grieve for you, father.
Kadmos:	I grieve for you too. And for your sisters.
Agave:	It is a terrible, terrible torment lord Dionysos has brought against our house.
Kadmos:	Terrible what you did to him. You took away the honour of his name in Thebes.
Agave:	Farewell, my father.
Kadmos:	Farewell, my poor dear daughter. But you are beyond faring well!
Agave:	Lead me away. To my sisters, to the place of our pitiful exile. May I never go near Kithairon again, never set eyes on it, never see a thyrsos, never remember a moment of this. Leave the thyrsos to the Bakkhai!

Bakkhai: Many are the forms of the *daimonic*
           and many the surprises wrought by gods.
           What seemed likely did not happen.
           But for the unexpected a god found a way.
           That's how this went
           today.